THEMES IN GEOGRAPHY

Rivers

FRED MARTIN

Heinemann

First published in Great Britain by Heinemann Library
Halley Court, Jordan Hill, Oxford OX2 8EJ
a division of Reed Educational & Professional Publishing Ltd

MELBOURNE AUCKLAND
FLORENCE PRAGUE MADRID ATHENS
SINGAPORE TOKYO CHICAGO SAO PAULO
PORTSMOUTH NH MEXICO
IBADAN GABORONE JOHANNESBURG
KAMPALA NAIROBI

Designed by Artistix
Originated by Dot Gradations Ltd., South Woodham Ferrers
Printed in the UK by Jarrold Book Printing Ltd., Thetford

00 99 98 97 96
10 9 8 7 6 5 4 3 2 1

ISBN 0 431 06441 5

British Library Cataloguing in Publication Data

Martin, Fred, 1948 –
    Rivers. – (Themes in geography)
    1. Rivers – Juvenile literature
    I. Title II. Series
    551.4'83

Acknowledgements
The Publishers would like to thank the following for permission to reproduce photographs.

Ace Photo Library/Geoff Smith: p.43. Ace Photo Library/Marka: p.11. Bruce Coleman/Andrew Davies: p.42. Bruce Coleman/Andy Purcell: p.34. Bruce Coleman/Chris James: p.16. Bruce Coleman/Christer Fredriksson: p.29. Bruce Coleman/David Davies: p.38. Bruce Coleman/Dr Eckart Pott: p.22. Bruce Coleman/F & P Bauer: p.45. Bruce Coleman/Gerald Cubitt: p.6. Bruce Coleman/Gordon Langsbury: p.33. Bruce Coleman/Hans Reinhard: p.14. Bruce Coleman/Janos Jurka: p.17. Bruce Coleman/John Shaw: p.44. Bruce Coleman/Jules Cowan: p.18. Bruce Coleman/Mark N Boulton: p.23. Cambridge University Museum of Archaeology and Anthropology: p.31. Celtic Picture Library: p.12. Cephas/Dorothy Burrows: p.5. Derek Pratt/Waterways Photo Library: p.30. Frank Lane/Fronts Hartmann: p.26. Frank Lane/Silvestria: p.10. Fred Martin: p.8, p.13, p.41. Magnum/Michael Nichols: p.21. Magnum/P Jones Griffiths: p.35. Nature Photographers/Andrew Cleave: p.19. Nature Photographers/EA James: p.20. NHPA/© ANT: p.15. Robert Harding Picture Library: p.27. Spectrum Colour Library: p.32, p.39. Still Pictures: p.9. Still Pictures/Herbert Giradet: p.7. Still Pictures/Jordan Schytte: p.40. Still Pictures/Mark Edwards: p.37. Still Pictures/Paul Harrison: p.25. Telegraph Colour Library/L Lefkowitz: p.36. Telegraph Colour Library/River Rooks: p.28. Telegraph Colour Library/Space Frontiers: p.24. Tony Stone Images: p.4.

Cover photograph reproduced with permission of The Image Bank.

Our thanks to Clare Boast, Sutherland Primary School, Stoke on Trent, for her comments in the preparation of this book.

Every effort has been made to contact copyright holders of any material reproduced in this book. Any omissions will be rectified in subsequent printings if notice is given to the Publisher.

Contents

Where rivers start

Rivers are always moving. Perhaps that is why they are so interesting to look at. They are always coming from somewhere and going somewhere else.

A river's source

Most of the world's longest rivers start in high mountain areas. The Missouri River for example, starts in the Rocky Mountains of North America. The Amazon begins in the Andes mountains of South America. The place where a river starts is called its **source**.

Rills and streams

A river's water comes from rain that falls on the mountains. Some of this quickly flows down the slopes into small **channels** called **rills**. The rills join each other until there is a **stream**. The streams join up until there is a river.

Melting snow and ice

Some of the water in rivers comes from melting snow and ice. Frozen snow and ice doesn't start melting off the mountain slopes until the weather becomes warmer. Sometimes, the ice moves as a **glacier** down a valley to where the air is warmer. This makes it melt. **Meltwater streams** then rush out from under the glacier to start a river. Rivers that flow from melting snow and ice can suddenly get much deeper and **flood** when the weather warms up and the snow melts.

The Rocky Mountains in Banff National Park, USA.

Water melts from the snow and ice to form a lake.

Water flows from the rocks at Goredale Scar in Yorkshire.

Rainwater sinks into the permeable limestone rock, then comes up as a spring.

A river flows from the spring.

Springs

Some rivers begin where water flows out of rocks. This happens at a **spring**. The River Thames starts this way. Rainwater sinks through soil and into the spaces in the rock below. Rock like this is said to be **permeable**. Chalk and sandstone are examples of permeable rocks.

The water sinks down until it reaches an **impermeable** layer that it cannot sink through. The water fills up spaces in the permeable rock up to a level called the **water table**.

Water flows out of the rocks when the water table is at the surface. This happens where a layer of rock is exposed on a slope.

A boggy start

In some places, rainwater cannot sink into the ground or flow quickly off the surface. Instead, it lies on the surface to form a bog.

The soil and vegetation soak up the water like a sponge. The water flows out of the bog to form streams and rivers. This is why the rivers keep flowing long after it has stopped raining.

Did you know?

The highest source of the River Nile was discovered in 1937 when Burkhart Waldecker reached a spring at the mouth of the Kagera River. The Kagera flows into Lake Victoria.

The Rivers Rhine and Rhone have their sources near each other in the Swiss Alps. The Rhine flows north into the North Sea. The Rhone flows south into the Mediterranean Sea.

Draining the land

Watch what happens to the ground when it rains. Soil and plants quickly become wet. In streets, the water stands as puddles, then runs into drains. Before long, the water has all gone. Some of it is on its way to rivers.

Rain into rivers

The type of ground affects the amount of water and the time it takes for rainwater to get to a river. Different types of slopes, soil, rock and vegetation all affect what happens.

Some rainwater runs down slopes and flows directly into streams and rivers. This is called **surface runoff**.

There is most surface runoff where slopes are steep and rocky. This water gets into a river very quickly. Another route rainwater can take is to flow through the soil and rocks before flowing into a river. This takes very much longer and the flow is spread over more time.

Grass and trees

Rain that falls on grass and trees takes much longer to get into a river. It stays on leaves and branches and only slowly drips to the ground. This is why the ground under a tree during a rainstorm can be drier than that around it.

Where there is little or no vegetation, the rainwater sinks quickly into the ground or flows as surface runoff.

A fast-flowing mountain river in the Himalayan Mountains, Nepal.

The trees soak up some of the rain and stop it from flowing as surface runoff.

Rivers as drains

Once the rainwater gets into a river, it quickly flows away from the area. This is how a river drains the water from an area where rain and snow has fallen. The area any river collects water from is called its **drainage basin.**

Water that evaporates

Not all rain and snow gets into rivers. On a warm day, water is heated until it turns back into a gas. This gas is called **water vapour.** The water is said to have **evaporated**.

The water vapour rises back into the air and forms clouds. It can then cool down and turn back to rain, or it can be blown to another area by the wind.

Water through roots

Rainwater helps plants to grow. Their roots suck water out of the ground. The water moves up a plant until it evaporates from the leaves. This is called **transpiration.** So the more plants there are in an area, the less rainwater is likely to reach a river.

Did you know?

The average depth of rainfall that falls on the River Thames drainage basin in a year is 716 mm. The average amount of runoff into the streams and rivers of the drainage basin is only 209 mm. This means that two thirds of the rain either evaporates or sinks deep into the rocks.

An area of cleared rain forest in Brazil.

Lack of trees means that more water will flow off the surface into rivers.

Tributaries

Most rivers start as a gentle trickle of water that flows from a **spring** or from a bog. By the time they reach the sea, most rivers are flowing in wide and deep **channels**. A lot of the extra water has come from smaller rivers and **streams** that join them.

Rills and streams

At first, rainwater flows in small channels called **rills** that are only a few centimetres deep and wide. Soon the rills flow into each other. This is how larger streams are formed.

The extra amount of water makes a stream's channel deeper and wider. The streams themselves become wider and deeper as they join with other streams. A stream that takes most of the water from an area becomes a river.

A tributary river

A river becomes even larger when another river flows into it. The water being drained from two areas now has to flow in one channel. A river that flows into a larger river is called a **tributary**.

Rainwater has cut small channels down the slope of this pile of soil.

The small channels are already joining each other to make larger channels.

Soil is washed away to make the channel deeper and wider.

The river Tocantins is one of the main Amazon tributaries. The Tocantins is itself joined by many smaller tributaries.

The brown colour is caused by mud that has been washed into the river where trees have been cut down for farming and mining.

A river's discharge

A river grows as more tributaries flow into it. The amount of water flowing in a river is called its **discharge**. The greater the discharge, the deeper or wider the river becomes.

Amazon tributaries

There is no special size a river needs to be to get called a tributary. All it has to do is flow into a larger river. Some of the world's longest rivers are joined by tributaries that are themselves major rivers.

The River Amazon is no bigger than any other stream near its source. The Amazon is fed by two **headwater rivers** named the Ucayali and the Maranon. These join near Nauta in Peru to become the Amazon.

As it flows through the rain forest, the Amazon is joined by major tributaries such as the Tocantins and the Negro. By the time the Amazon enters the Atlantic Ocean, it has drained an area that is 6 million square kilometres. This is larger than the whole continent of Europe.

Did you know?

The River Amazon has a discharge of between 9 and 32 million gallons every second as it enters the Atlantic Ocean.

The amount of fresh water that flows into the ocean from the Amazon is about 20% of all the fresh water that flows into the oceans.

Great rivers

Of all the water in the world, very little is flowing in rivers at any one time. About three quarters of the world's water is salt water in the seas and oceans. Only 0.01% is fresh water in rivers and lakes.

Record rivers

There are different ways to measure the size of a river. One way is to measure its length from its **source** to its mouth. The **mouth** is where it flows out to the sea.

A river's length cannot be measured as a straight line. Rivers flow in great bends called **meanders**. This adds to the distance the river has to flow.

The river's **discharge** is another way to measure its size. The discharge increases until it reaches its mouth. An average figure is usually given because the discharge varies during the year.

The size of rivers can also be compared by measuring the sizes of the areas they drain. This includes all the areas that are drained by **tributaries**. This total area is called a river's **drainage basin** or **catchment area**.

Rivers in history

Some of the oldest cities and civilizations have grown beside rivers. This happened in Egypt, India and China where great civilizations developed in river valleys. The flat land and rich soil was good for farming. People could also use the rivers to transport goods. Seventeenth-century explorers used the St Lawrence River as a way of getting further into North America. It was easier than going through the forests.

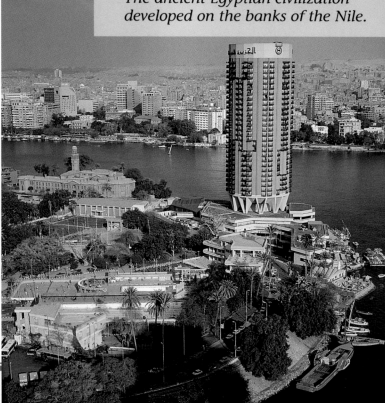

The River Nile is the world's longest river at 6690 km.

The ancient Egyptian civilization developed on the banks of the Nile.

Did you know?

Longest rivers of the world

Name	Outflow	Length in miles	Length in kilometres
Nile	Mediterranean Sea	4132	6650
Amazon – Ucayali – Apurimac	South Atlantic Ocean	4000	6400
Yangtze	East China Sea	3915	6300
Mississippi – Missouri – Red Rock	Gulf of Mexico	3710	5971
Yenisey – Baikal – Selenga	Kara Sea	3442	5540
Whang He (Yellow)	Gulf of Chihli	3395	5464
Ob – Irtysh	Gulf of Ob	3362	5410
Páraná	Rio de la Plata	3032	4880
Congo	South Atlantic Ocean	2900	4700
Amur – Argun	Sea of Okhotsk	2761	4444

Great rivers today

Many of the world's great rivers are still important for transport and other purposes. Most of them have been changed in some way by people. The Mississippi has been made straighter and deeper so that boats can carry goods up and down its length. A **dam** has been built across the River Nile at Aswan to create electricity.

Water is taken out of rivers for people to drink and to water crops. In Asia, so much water has been taken out of the rivers Amu and Syr for irrigation that the Aral Sea they flow into is in danger of drying up completely.

One of the greatest problems is how to control the great rivers and stop them from flooding. The power of the great rivers has proved hard to tame.

The Amazon as it enters the ocean.

The Amazon is the world's second longest river at 6650 km.

Out of the mouth

A river ends when it flows into another river, the sea or sometimes into a lake. The place where this happens is called the river's **mouth**. This is where all the water, as well as all the mud and **pollution**, reach the end of their river journey.

A river estuary

For most rivers, the river's mouth opens into a sea or ocean. The River Rhine for example, flows into the North Sea.

Most rivers slowly become wider as they flow towards and then into the sea. This wider area near a river mouth is called an **estuary**. It is here that the river flow meets the **tidal** waters from the sea. The River Severn in England, for example, has an estuary that widens out to 2 km as it enters the Bristol Channel.

As a river flows into the sea, it drops the mud it is carrying on its **bed** and along its **banks**. When the tide goes out, wide areas of this deposited river mud are left exposed. These areas are called **mudflats**.

The River Conway in North Wales flows into the Irish Sea.

Conway Castle was built by Edward I in about 1280. The bridge was built in 1827 by Thomas Telford.

The estuary of the River Severn.

The difference between high and low tide in the Severn estuary is about 14 metres. This is the world's second biggest difference between high and low tide.

Tidal waters

Salt water from the oceans comes some way up an estuary at each high tide. The stretch of a river where this happens is said to be **tidal**.

At times when there is a special high tide, sea water rushes up the estuary like water flowing up a funnel. This causes a special high wave called a **bore**. Surfers and canoeists often wait for a bore so they can ride it upstream.

Inland drainage

Some rivers end in lakes or seas that are below the normal sea level. There is no route from here to the open sea as water cannot flow uphill. These are areas where there is **inland drainage**.

Forming rocks

The mud, sand and gravel carried by rivers is washed along the coast and out to sea. Layers of these materials heap up on top of each other. Each layer becomes more squashed by the weight of the layers above. This is one way that, over millions of years, new rocks are formed. Rocks formed in this way are called **sedimentary rocks**. This is because they have been formed from small pieces called sediment.

Did you know?

The Caspian Sea is an area of inland drainage. It is about 28 metres below sea level.

Sedimentary rocks from the bed of an ancient ocean are now part of Mount Everest, the world's highest mountain.

Mountain streams

Mountains last for tens of millions of years. But no matter how high or how strong they are, all mountains are worn down over time.

River erosion

A river cuts a **channel** into the ground as soon as it starts to flow. The bottom of the channel is called the river's **bed**. The sides of the channel are the **banks**.

Small pieces of loose rock are soon carried away. Rock is also made smooth as water and stones wash over it. This wearing away of the landscape is called **erosion**.

A mountain valley

A mountain **valley** often has very steep sides, like a 'V' shape. A deep notch is formed as fast-flowing water carries away pieces of broken rock. The rain washes more soil and rock down the valley slopes. The river also carries this away. This is how a valley is formed.

A steep-sided mountain valley being eroded by a fast-flowing stream.

The river is cutting down into the hard rock and slowly removing it.

Blocks of rock break off the valley sides and roll down into the river bed. These are broken up and washed away by the force of the river.

Valley spurs

It is hard to see straight up a mountain valley. The view is blocked by ridges of rock that jut out from the sides. These are called valley **spurs**. They form because the river takes a winding, rather than a straight course. In time, the spurs will be worn away as the river makes its valley lower and wider.

The power to erode

A river needs **energy** to do its work of erosion. It gets its energy from the speed of the water as it flows down towards the sea. The river's slope is called the **gradient**. As **tributaries** join the main river, there is even more force of water to cause even more erosion.

Glaciers

Rivers are not the only force that shape mountain valleys. During the last **Ice Age**, **glaciers** moved down mountain valleys and changed their shape. Valleys were made wider and deeper, and their sides were made straighter. When the ice melted, rivers started to flow again.

Did you know?

The River Ganges in India carries 1500 million tonnes of soil and small pieces of rock towards the sea each year. Much of this has come from the Himalayan Mountains.

Steep 'V'-shaped valleys in the Bogong National Park in Victoria, Australia.

Spurs make it impossible to have a clear view up the valley.

The whole landscape is slowly being eroded by the streams and rivers.

Waterfalls and rapids

Waterfalls are some of the most spectacular sights in the natural landscape. Tourists stand and stare as an endless torrent of water crashes down. Yet they are features in the landscape that do not last for long.

Hard rock layers

A waterfall is where a river drops vertically to a lower level. Most waterfalls are in the upper part of a river's course as it flows through mountains.

There is often a waterfall where a river finds it hard to cut down into a more **resistant** rock. This can be where a river crosses from one type of rock onto another.

The river wears down faster into the less resistant rock, but the more resistant rock above slows down the amount of **erosion**. The difference in the amount of erosion creates a waterfall.

Glaciers and waterfalls

Some waterfalls have been caused by glaciers. During the last **Ice Age**, **glaciers** cut deep **valleys** into the mountains. Larger valleys were cut by larger glaciers. This has left smaller valleys hanging above the larger valleys. Waterfalls now mark the places where the smaller valleys join the larger and deeper glacial valleys.

Thornton Force waterfall in Yorkshire.

A hard layer of rock on top is overhanging a softer layer beneath.

White-water rafting on rapids in Sweden.

Rivers in Sweden fall steeply to the coast from mountains where there are large amounts of rain and snow.

Moving back

Water tumbling over a waterfall falls with great force. Stones and other pieces of rock are carried with it. This cuts out a **plunge hole** at the bottom of the waterfall.

Did you know?

Angel Falls in Venezuela is the world's highest waterfall at 979 metres.

Niagara Falls between the USA and Canada is divided into two parts. The Horseshoe Falls has a drop of 49 metres. The American Falls drops 51 metres.

The Horseshoe Falls is wearing back at 1.5 metres each year on average. It has eroded back by 11 km in the last 12,000 years.

Water also cuts back into softer rock under the waterfall. As it does this, the upper layers are left unsupported, so the face of the waterfall collapses. Then the undercutting starts again. Each time this happens, the waterfall moves back upstream. When the layer of resistant rock is completely gone, the waterfall will no longer exist.

White-water fun

Rapids are places where the river drops quickly, but not steeply enough to be called a waterfall. They form where a layer of resistant rock stops the river from cutting down a flatter, more even slope in its **bed**.

Large boulders make rapids dangerous for boats, though the sport of **white-water rafting** has become very popular. Rapids, like waterfalls, only remain until the river manages to wear away the more resistant rock.

Canyons and gorges

There are places where rivers have cut deep gashes in the landscape. These features are called **canyons** and **gorges**. The steep slopes and rushing water show the power of natural forces to erode the landscape.

The Grand Canyon

The Grand Canyon in the USA is the world's deepest, longest and widest canyon. It stretches for 350 km, at times reaching 25 km wide. The sides drop steeply. In some sections, the sides go straight down for 1620 metres.

The history of the Earth's rocks is shown in layers down the canyon sides. Each different colour and change in slope shows a different layer of rock. The youngest rocks are towards the top. Some of the earth's oldest rocks are exposed at the bottom.

Cutting the Grand Canyon

The Grand Canyon has been cut by the Colorado River. The river has cut down deeply through the rocks. Small pieces are still being broken off and carried away by the fast-flowing river. This helps explain why the colour of the Colorado River is often red.

But while the river is cutting down, the land in this part of the USA is rising. This makes the river cut down even more and stops it from making the canyon much wider.

The Horseshoe Bend in the Colorado River, Arizona, USA.

Limestone gorges

In some deep and narrow gorges you can find the **sedimentary rock** called limestone. One reason for this is that most rainwater sinks through limestone. This means that the landscape in a limestone area is not affected by the usual types of **erosion** on the surface. A river passing through the area is likely to cut a gorge and not a wider valley, or even flow beneath the surface as an underground river.

Some limestone gorges have been formed when the roof of a cave that an underground river runs through has collapsed.

Desert wadis

Some canyons and gorges are in deserts. These are called **wadis**. It is unusual to see water flowing through them as there is so little rain in a desert. Many thousands of years ago, the Earth's climate was different from today. Places that are desert now were much wetter then. Wadis were cut when there was enough rain to let rivers flow.

Did you know?

The Colorado River gets its name from a Spanish word that means the colour red.

Rocks at the bottom of the Grand Canyon are from a time in our past called the Pre-Cambrian period. These rocks are at least 2000 million years old!

A limestone gorge in Yorkshire.

This gorge may be a cave that has collapsed.

Rivers in caves

Rivers flow under the ground as well as on the surface. This happens in areas where the rock is so **permeable** that rainwater sinks through it. Whole rivers can disappear below ground when they reach this type of rock. Once underground, rivers carry on flowing. This is how some caves are formed.

Limestone landscapes

Most caves are in areas where there are thick layers of limestone rock. Rainwater is able to dissolve limestone. It does this by picking up the carbon dioxide gas from the air. This makes the rain act in the same way as a weak acid, which can eat away at the rock, weakening and then destroying it.

Cracks in the limestone become wider as the rock is dissolved. Some become so wide that they are known as **swallow holes** or **sink holes**.

Rivers and caves

Rainwater flows down through these cracks. Then it flows along cracks between different layers of the limestone. The cracks become wider as even more water flows along them.

The flowing water forms underground rivers. An underground river is able to erode a cave out of the limestone.

An area of limestone rock in Yorkshire.

Rainwater sinks through cracks to flow underground.

Stalactites and stalagmites

Inside a limestone cave, water drips down through the roof from above. Pieces of the dissolved limestone become solid again as the water hangs on the roof. This makes pointed shapes of limestone called **stalactites** that hang from the roof, and **stalagmites** that grow up from where the drips fall on the cave floor.

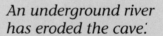

The Lechuguilla cave system in New Mexico, USA.

An underground river has eroded the cave.

Stalactites and stalagmites grow as water containing dissolved limestone drips through the cave.

A dangerous hobby

Many people enjoy exploring caves as a hobby. They squeeze through narrow cracks to try to find new caves. They use underwater equipment to swim and find out exactly where underground rivers go. People have to be rescued from caves every year. This is usually because of unexpected rain that makes the underground rivers suddenly rise. An underground river usually comes to the surface through a **spring** or a cave entrance.

Did you know?

The Echo River flows through the Mammoth Caves in Kentucky at a depth of 110 metres below ground.

The study of caves is called speleology.

A river valley

As a river flows towards the sea, it moves down through hills and on to even lower land called a **plain**. A plain is usually a wide river valley formed over a very long period of time. It can be so wide that it is impossible to see the opposite sides.

Down to sea level

Rivers erode the land they flow through. The landscape is also changed by the wind, and by moving ice such as **glaciers** and ice sheets. Along the coast, waves cause **erosion**. These are all known as **agents of erosion**. The main type of erosion in each area depends on the climate.

Rivers cannot go below sea level because they cannot flow uphill. By the time they are flowing in a lowland area, there is not much further down they can erode.

Widening a valley

Rivers use their energy to erode sideways when they are near to sea level. They snake from one side of their valley to the other. The bends in a river's course are called **meanders**.

The meanders make the **valley** bottom wider by wearing away any ridges of land that jut out. This helps straighten out the valley's sides.

The Wild River in Glacier National Park, USA.

The river is meandering and making its valley wider.

Stumps of hard rock will be worn back in time.

The flood plain of the River Severn at Gloucester.

The flat valley plain has been flooded after heavy winter rain and melting snow.

A river flood plain

Meandering makes the bottom of a valley almost flat. This is because the river wears away everything in its path, no matter how resistant it is.

The flat shape is also because the river drops mud it has been carrying. This happens after a **flood** as the floodwater sinks into the valley bottom and drains back into the river's channel. This area is called the river's **flood plain**.

The mud is dropped because the river is not flowing fast enough to carry it any more. The river mud also helps to make the soil fertile. Farmers do not like floods, but they like the new soil that is left behind.

Gentle slopes

The slopes of a lowland valley are worn down by small **streams** that flow down their sides. These flow into the valley bottom then join the main river as **tributaries**. Rain washes soil down the slopes. Hollows are filled in until the sides slope gently down to the flood plain.

Did you know?

The flood plain of the Mississippi Valley reaches a width of about 120 km.

The fine mud dropped by a river is called silt.

Delta landscapes

In ancient Greek, a letter shaped like a triangle was called delta. In geography, the word now means something different. Since the mouth of some rivers is 'D' shaped, this shape is called a **delta**.

Delta shapes

Most of the world's largest rivers have a delta at their **mouth**. The Mississippi, Ganges, Amazon and Nile all have deltas. Some deltas are shaped like an arc. Others look like a set of fingers, or like a bird's foot. These are called **bird's foot deltas**.

Islands and creeks

The landscape in a delta is very flat. Small **streams**, also known as creeks, flow through it. These streams are formed when a river splits up to flow between the islands of mud. In the USA, the streams that flow through the Mississippi delta are called **bayous**.

The highest point in a delta is never much more than the highest level of the sea. Low islands made entirely from mud take shape. The ground on some islands can become firm enough for people to live on.

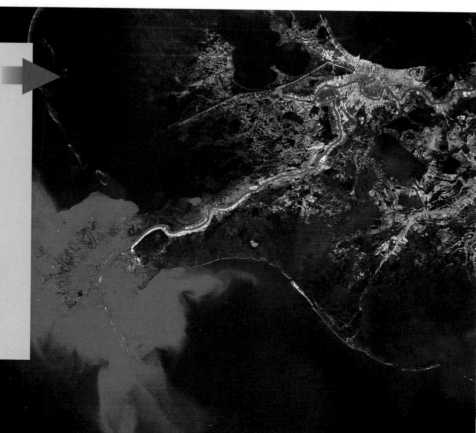

The Mississippi delta flows into the Gulf of Mexico.

The Mississippi River has a bird's foot delta.

Blue shows where the river is carrying mud right out into the Gulf of Mexico.

The flat delta land in Bangladesh at the mouth of the Ganges.

Grasses take root and change the mud into soil.

Taking root

The mud that forms a delta is carried there by the river. It is dropped when the river slows down as it flows into the sea. The mud is only carried along while the river is moving fairly fast.

Grasses and other types of marsh vegetation that can survive in the **tidal** salt water take root in the mud. This helps protect the mud from being washed away by waves and sea currents. They also trap more mud. The rotting vegetation helps change the mud into soil.

Inland deltas

A delta can form in any place where a river carrying mud or stones suddenly slows down. This does not have to be on the coast. It can be where a river enters a lake or sometimes where one river flows into another.

Did you know?

Some of the world's worst flood disasters have happened in the Ganges delta. People who live on the low islands are at risk from both river floods and waves caused by cyclones. In 1990, 140,000 people were killed during one cyclone.

The Nile delta is in danger of being washed away by the sea. This is because a *dam* across the Nile at Aswan is stopping much of the river mud from reaching the delta.

River erosion

Nothing can survive being scraped and rubbed forever. This is what flowing water does to the **bed** and **banks** of a river **channel**. It takes time to do this, but there is no shortage of time!

Eroding the banks

The force of the flowing water is enough to wash away loose soil and rock from a river's banks. **Erosion** at the bottom of the bank leaves the top part with no support. The unsupported bank soon collapses.

Material that collapses is quickly washed away. This allows the water to get at the bank again.

Look for evidence

Evidence for river bank erosion is often easy to see. Tree roots are left exposed as the bank is worn back into the **valley** bottom.

Cracks in the soil appear along the top of the bank near the edge. This shows that the ground beneath has been worn away and that the bank is about to collapse. Sometimes whole clumps of soil with grass still growing on top can be seen in the water.

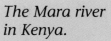

The Mara river in Kenya.

Erosion is washing soil from the outside of a bend.

Trees in the water show that part of the bank has collapsed.

Some parts of the bank are left with nothing underneath.

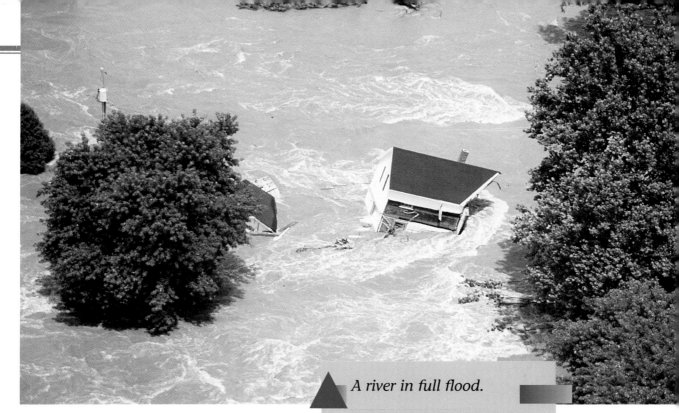

A river in full flood.

The force of the flowing water is powerful enough to carry away a house.

Rubbing and scraping

The river bed itself is also eroded and made deeper. Most erosion of this type is caused by stones as they are carried along in the current.

A river loaded with stones causes far more erosion than one that is carrying mud. The action is like rubbing sandpaper against wood. This action is called **corrasion**. Stones rub and scrape against the **bedrock** that forms the river bed.

Some stones are caught in swirls of water that move them around in a circle. This drills out holes called **potholes**. The potholes can become so big that they join each other. Potholes are another way that the river's bed is made lower.

The power to erode

Much of the erosion happens when the river is in **flood**. This is when it flows at its highest level and its fastest speed. The faster the flow, the more **energy** the river has to erode its banks.

Did you know?

Rivers do three types of work. They wear away a landscape by erosion. They transport the eroded material away. Then they deposit what they have transported.

Moving the load

Rivers are like conveyor belts. They move soil and rock from one place to another without stopping. Pieces are picked up and dropped off all along the way. The journey comes to an end when the river enters the sea. The job of moving something from one place to another is called transporting.

Types of load

The name given to all the material that is transported is called the river's load. The largest pieces are boulders.

Some get there when rocks break off a steep **valley** side and tumble to the bottom. Other pieces are broken off the river's **bed** and **banks**.

Smaller stones are also carried along. Some were larger pieces that smashed into each other and became smaller. The smallest pieces end up as grains of sand.

A mountain stream in British Columbia, Canada.

Large boulders are part of the river's load. The boulders have been rounded by the water and by rolling along the river's bed.

Rivers in Costa Rica carrying different types of load.

Stones and gravel are carried by one of the rivers.

The brown colour shows that one of the rivers is carrying a large amount of eroded soil.

Bumping and rolling

The largest pieces of rock are pushed along by the strength of the river's current. These can weigh several tonnes. It takes a very fast flow to do this.

Some boulders stay in the same place for several years. They do not move until there is very heavy rain and the river flows much faster than normal. Then they are rolled along until they come to a stop again. As they roll, sharp edges are broken off and they become smaller. This helps them to roll even further.

Suspended mud

Small pieces of mud are carried along suspended in the water. This happens as long as the river flow is fast enough to keep them from sinking down to the river bed. Soil is also carried along. This can change the colour of a river.

Some rocks will dissolve in water. The dissolved material is carried along in the water with the rest of the river's load. The Mississippi River carries about 200 million tonnes of dissolved material every year.

Did you know?

The Whang He river in China is also called the Yellow River. It gets its yellow colour from the fine yellow soil it picks up on one part of its journey.

During one flood at Lynmouth in Devon, 100,000 tonnes of boulders were moved and dropped on the floor of the valley. The river that did this flows for less than 10 km from the Exmoor uplands.

Meandering rivers

First tie a length of rope at one end. Then shake the rope so that it moves like a snake. The rope looks as if it is moving forwards, but it is only the bends you have made that move. A river's **meanders** move in the same kind of way.

A meandering habit

A river does not flow in a straight line. The word used to describe a river's course is meandering.

In the mountains, the whole **valley** winds as the river cuts a course through the softest bits of ground on its way towards the sea. In lowland areas where the valley bottom is wider, the river carries on meandering from side to side.

A meander bend can take the river all the way from one side of the valley bottom to the other. All rivers meander in this way. Rivers only flow straight where people have built concrete **banks**.

Meander loops

Some meander bends grow to become giant loops. A **meander neck** is the narrow piece of land between the start and end of a meander bend. The neck of a meander can be so narrow that the river eventually breaks through it.

The valley sides are being worn away on the outside of each meander bend.

Stones, gravel and sand are deposited on the inside front of the meander bend.

A meander bend of the River Thames in London.

The river's meanders have made the valley bottom flat.

Mud and gravel have been dropped on the valley floor. This made it easy to dig out London's old dockland area.

Breaking the neck

A meander neck is sometimes broken when the river is in **flood**. This leaves the loop without any water flowing into it.

At first, a lake called an **ox-bow lake** is formed. It is called an ox-bow lake because it is shaped like the old-fashioned 'U'-shaped yoke that was used to hitch an ox to a plough. The lake lasts until it becomes overgrown with weeds and filled in with soil.

Moving meanders

A river always flows fastest on the outside of a meander bend. It has furthest to go around the outside and the force of the current takes the water there. This means there is more **erosion** on the outside.

On the inside of the bend, the flow is slower. Because the river is moving more slowly, sand and stones are dropped there. It can look like a beach on the inside of a meander bend.

Meander bends move across the valley by eroding on one side and dropping the load on the other. In time, meanders work their way over all parts of the valley floor. This helps explain why valley **flood plains** are usually so flat.

Did you know?

Another word for an ox-bow lake is a mort lake. This is because 'mort' is the French word for dead. The lake 'dies' because no more water flows into it.

River flow

The amount of water that flows down a river changes often. At one extreme, there is so much water that it bursts its **banks** and **floods**. At other times, the same river can dry up.

Rain and river flow

The amount of water flowing in a river is called its **discharge**. This is usually measured by the number of cubic metres that flow past a point in one second.

The discharge goes up and down throughout the year. This is because there are different amounts of rain in the river's **drainage basin** at different times of the year.

High flow

In the UK, there is usually more rain in the winter months so rivers are at their highest. Winter months are also colder. Less water on the ground is **evaporated** when it is colder. This allows more water to flow as **surface runoff**.

Low flow

The total amount of rain that falls in the summer is usually less than in winter. Warmer temperatures mean that more rainwater is evaporated so it does not get to the rivers. There is more vegetation to hold back the rain. However, summer rainstorms can be quite violent and can make small rivers rise very quickly.

The River Thames at Abingdon in Oxfordshire during the summer.

The water level is near the top of the banks but this is a low flow period with little risk of a flood.

Melting snow

Spring is a dangerous season in places where rivers come from high mountain areas. During the winter, water has fallen as snow instead of rain. Snow lies on the ground, some of it turning into ice.

The River Thames in Berkshire has burst its banks and flooded nearby homes.

When the weather becomes warmer, snow and ice begin to melt. Heavy rain at the same time can add so much extra water to the river that it can cause a flood.

The Nile

A river's flow in any one place depends on where the water has come from. The River Nile gets some of its water from Lake Victoria on the equator where there is always some rain. This branch of the Nile is called the White Nile.

Further north, a tributary called the Blue Nile flows down from the Ethiopian mountains. This brings most water between July and November.

This is why the Nile's flow of water north of the Sudanese city of Khartoum, where the Blue and While Niles meet, changes so much from one season to the other.

Dried up springs

After a long period with little or no rain, the level of water in rocks can sink so low that **springs** dry up. This can make rivers stop flowing.

Did you know?

The average discharge of the River Thames over the whole year is about 70 cubic metres per second. Its greatest recorded discharge is about 1060 cubic metres per second.

River floods

Living close to a river is a risk. The risk is that the river will **flood**. All rivers flood from time to time. The only questions are when and how deep and dangerous the floodwaters will be.

Too much rain

Most floods happen when there is much more rain than usual. After days or weeks of above average rain, the ground becomes **saturated** with water. No more rain is able to soak into saturated ground. Any more rain has to flow off the surface as runoff. It does this quickly so the level of water in a river rises rapidly and causes a flood.

On some **tidal** rivers, there is an extra problem when there is a high tide. A high tide at the same time as high rainfall can make a river flood. The two events are not connected so it is just bad luck.

Snow and rain

Melting snow is another cause of river floods. The worst problems come when there is heavy rain at the same time as quickly melting snow.

This sometimes happens when air from the Atlantic Ocean blows over the UK after a long cold period. Snow on the mountains starts to melt. Rain comes in with the milder Atlantic air. The extra amount of water is too much for the rivers to take.

The River Avon in Gloucestershire.

The Avon is a tributary of the River Severn.

Heavy rain and melting snow in January 1991 caused the river to rise over its banks.

The town of Hannibal, Missouri, USA, during the Mississippi floods of 1993.

Forty-five people were killed by the 1993 floods.

There was damage to 30,000 homes because of floodwater.

Damage to farmland and other property worth at least $10 billion was caused by the flood.

Flooding the land

Once floodwater spills onto the flat **valley** bottom, there is nothing to stop it spreading. In the Mississippi floods of 1993, floodwater spread out for 10 km. Fields were covered by water that was 3 metres deep. The wider and flatter the **flood plain**, the further the water is able to spread.

Flash floods

Some floods come without warning. This happens in places that are usually so hot and dry that rivers do not usually flow at all. A sudden cloudburst can be enough to quickly fill dried up river **channels**. Rain runs off the surface into these channels. There is little vegetation or soil to soak it up. The result is a **flash flood** that nobody can predict.

Did you know?

Some scientists believe there will be more floods because of global warming. Warmer climates should mean less rain in total, but there will be more violent weather and rainstorms. The polar ice caps could also start to melt.

In October 1994, four British tourists were killed by a flash flood on the Greek island of Rhodes. The road collapsed and a flood swept their car away.

Dams and reservoirs

Water in rivers is too useful for us to let it all flow out to the sea. It is needed to drink, for growing crops, in factories and for many other reasons. The problem is that a river does not always give the right amount of water at the right time. Building a **dam** and a **reservoir** is one solution to this problem.

Building a dam

A dam makes sure that water from wet months can be stored for months that are dry. It also helps stop **floods**.

In India, some dams are a low bank across a **stream**. These are built from soil and rock by local village people. Dams can also be giant concrete walls. The Chicasen Dam in Mexico is 261 metres high.

A reservoir

A reservoir is an artificial lake that floods the land behind a dam. Some of the world's largest lakes are reservoirs. Lake Nasser behind the Aswan dam across the river Nile in Egypt is 500 km long. It covers an area of 5000 km^2.

The right place

The best place to build a dam is where the river flows through a narrow **valley**. The dam can be short and the valley sides make a natural wall.

The Glen Canyon Dam across the Colorado River in Arizona, USA.

The dam is 216 metres high and 475 metres wide.

Building a new dam in Panama.

The narrow valley and hard rock makes this site suitable to build the dam.

Mountain areas are also best because of the high rainfall. Water collected like this may have to be moved by pipeline or canal to cities in the lowlands where it is needed.

Did you know?

A canal built to carry water is called an aqueduct.

One of the world's biggest dam schemes is in China on the Yangtze River. Fourteen million people have to be moved because of the dam and the new reservoir. The scheme will not be finished until the year 2010.

The flow of the River Euphrates in Turkey was stopped for 1 month in 1990 so that a reservoir could fill up behind a new dam.

Water for crops and power

Water from a reservoir can be used in different ways. Farmers can use the water for their crops. This is called **irrigation**.

A dam can be used to generate electricity. The force of rushing water is used to generate the electricity. A power station that works like this is called a **hydro-electric power station**.

Effects on rivers

Water supply, irrigation and power stations all affect the flow of water in a river. There is less water left in a river if it is used to irrigate crops and to provide drinking water. Another benefit of using and controlling a river's flow is that there is less chance of a flood.

Rivers and boats

Rivers were important for travel long before roads. Travel by boat was faster, more could be carried, and there was less chance of being stopped by robbers.

A navigable river

A river that can be used by boats is said to be **navigable**. A barge can travel up the Rhine from the port of Rotterdam at its **mouth**, to Basle in Switzerland. This is a distance of 800 km. The Mississippi River and its **tributaries** provide almost 20,000 km of navigable waterways in the USA.

Locks and weirs

Some rivers have to be changed to make them navigable. A **lock** and **weir** system is needed where the river's **gradient** is steep and the water flows too quickly. The weir is a small step built across the river. Boats are lifted up or down to a new level in the lock.

Barge traffic on the River Rhine in Germany.

The Rhine is one of Europe's busiest waterways.

A lock and weir on the River Thames at Goring in Oxfordshire.

A modern cabin cruiser moves out of the lock. Older narrow barges are tied up on the bank.

In 1990, an old canal was reopened that links the River Thames to the River Avon. This allows boats to travel from London to Bristol.

Dredging out

A river can be made deeper by **dredging** or blasting out mud and rock. This is what is happening to the River Araguaia in Brazil. Ships will be able to sail 1700 km from the town of Aruana to the port of Belem at the mouth of the Amazon.

Canalized

Some rivers such as the Mississippi have been made shorter and straighter by cutting off **meanders**. The **banks** are then made stronger to stop **erosion**.

These changes make the river more like a canal. A river where this is done is said to be **canalized**. Much of the river Moselle in France and Germany has been canalized so that barges can carry goods between the two countries.

Boating for pleasure

People also use boats for pleasure. Small cabin cruisers, yachts and rowing boats are a common sight on rivers. In the UK, rivers in the the Norfolk Broads are popular places for boating holidays. Even rivers in mountain areas can be used for leisure. Canoeists make use of their fast-flowing currents and **rapids**.

Did you know?

In 1992, a canal was opened that allows barges to travel between the River Rhine and the River Danube. A boat can now travel from the North Sea to the Black Sea, a distance of about 2000 km.

Flood defences

River **valleys** are some of the most densely populated places on Earth. Most major cities have been built next to rivers, either inland or on the coast. Although everyone knows that rivers can **flood**, people are still killed and property is still lost in river floods every year.

Raising levees

One of the oldest ways to stop floods is to make the river **banks** higher. Higher banks mean that more water is kept in the river's **channel**.

A narrow ridge along the top of a bank is called a **levee**. A levee is formed naturally from mud and soil along some rivers. A levee can be made higher with sand bags, rock and soil.

A levee has to be strong enough to stop the river breaking through it. Concrete may be needed along the river banks to stop this from happening.

There are two problems with raising levees. One is to know how high to raise them. The second is that if they work, the river is likely to flood somewhere else further downstream.

Building an earth bank to stop flooding in Bangladesh.

Women are doing the work using only simple tools.

There are 110 million people living in Bangladesh. Most of the country is flat and near to sea level.

The Ganges and Brahmaputra flow into the sea through Bangladesh. Heavy monsoon rains often cause flooding in both of these rivers.

Clearing the channel

Some river channels become clogged with mud and stones. This means there is less space for the extra flood water. A small **dam** can be built to trap stones and to stop them from moving downstream. More space can be made by dredging out the mud and stones. This helps keep more water in the river channel.

Planting trees

Floods happen when too much rainwater and melting snow gets into a river too quickly. There is not much that anyone can do about the weather, but planting trees stops too much water getting into a river in such a short time. Unfortunately, people have been cutting down more trees than have been replanted.

Don't live there!

Every method of stopping flooding is expensive and none of them lasts forever. Perhaps the best answer is to make sure that people do not live in places that are likely to be flooded. This is not easy to do because so many people live there already. They would have to find somewhere else to go.

Did you know?

There are just over 3500 km of raised levees along the Mississippi and its main *tributaries*.

In the UK, only 10% of the land is covered by trees. Settlements and roads with *impermeable* surfaces cover 16%.

A small river in the English Lake District.

A new channel has been made to contain flood water.

Stones are trapped then taken out of the river.

Dirty rivers

Rivers are nature's way of draining rain from the land. Unfortunately, people also use rivers as drains. They use them to drain away waste.

Spreading disease

Animals and people use rivers for drinking, washing, and sometimes also as a toilet. This allows disease to pass from person to person. The problem is worst in the world's poorest countries where drinking water supplies often come from rivers.

Factories and mines

Rivers become dirty when they are **polluted** by waste from factories. Waste chemicals are sometimes emptied into **streams** and rivers, though there are usually laws to stop this being done.

Waste water from old coal, lead and tin mines has become a special problem in the UK. Once the mine has closed, pumps that kept the mine dry are turned off. Water drips through the rocks and fills the mine shafts and tunnels.

By the time it comes to the surface through **springs**, the water has become polluted by the metal and by rusty machinery.

Pollution from an old coal mine in South Wales.

Almost all the coal mines in South Wales have been closed, but water still drips down through the rocks into the mines and out into local rivers.

Dead fish in a river that has been seriously polluted.

Farm waste

Farmers cause river pollution in places where they depend on chemicals to stop plant diseases, kill insects and act as fertilizers. Nitrates used to make the soil fertile are a special problem. These chemicals are washed into streams and rivers when it rains. The chemicals then affect the river's plant and animal life.

Did you know?

In 1994, cyanide killed every fish along a 6 mile stretch in the River Wye in Buckinghamshire.

The Mississippi River and Missouri River, as well as many others, are on a list of 'endangered' rivers in the USA. These are rivers that are seriously polluted by farm waste, boats, mining and untreated city waste.

In the UK, 90% of rivers are classed as having good to fair water quality. The rest do not.

If one type of plant or animal is harmed, others can also be affected. This is because different animals and fish feed on each other. This is called a **food chain**. If there is less of one type of plant or animal, then there is less food for another to live on.

Cleaning it up

Efforts are being made to clean up rivers that are polluted. Water companies are spending money to clean up the rivers. There are fines for people who deliberately cause pollution in rivers. This is a battle that has to be won if water is to be safe for both people and wildlife.

Rivers and nature

Rivers are the natural home for many kinds of fish, birds, insects and other animals. They are also where unique types of vegetation grow.

River habitats

Wildlife such as ducks and beavers have their homes along river **banks**. Reeds and other plants that grow near the banks provide a habitat for these animals. Reeds also help stop river bank **erosion**.

Other animals need rivers as a place to come and drink. In parts of Africa, herds of antelope, wildebeest, lions and elephants can all be seen drinking at rivers.

Conserving habitats

A wildlife habitat can easily be destroyed by the many ways that people use rivers. Draining and protecting land that sometimes **floods** also destroys rare habitats. It is important that more of these places are **conserved**.

Breaking the chain

Birds such as the kingfisher depend on small fish for their food. Others live off the millions of insects that live beside a river. Most of the animals are linked in a **food chain** in which one species feeds on another or on plants. If one part of the food chain is broken, there is an effect on all the other parts.

A clean mountain stream starting its journey to the sea.

The stream and river banks make a habitat for many types of wildlife.

*Fish can be used to give you a sign that a river is clean or **polluted**. For example, salmon will not swim up a polluted river.*

Fishing in a mountain stream in the Yellowstone National Park, USA.

Rivers have to be kept clean so that fish and other species can live in them.

Did you know?

In the UK, laws were made to stop lead being used as fishing weights. In 1994, five out of ten dead swans taken from the River Avon at Stratford were found to have died because of lead poisoning. This could be because they are still swallowing weights lost in the river before the law was made.

Fishing is the world's most popular hobby. There are 66 million anglers in the USA and 23 million in Japan. In the UK, at least 3 million people fish in rivers.

Fishing

Many people enjoy fishing as a hobby. In the past, lead used as line weights caused problems to birds such as swans who swallowed them and then slowly died of lead poisoning. Lines and nets can also cause problems if they are left to entangle birds and fish.

People who fish say their hobby helps keep rivers clean and helps to protect fish. They say that fish do not suffer pain when they are hooked then put back again. Others think that fishing is a cruel sport that ought to be stopped.

Learning to enjoy

To protect each species, it is important to conserve the whole river environment. Knowing something about rivers should help you to protect and enjoy them even more.

Glossary

agents of erosion those forces which cause erosion, such as water, ice, wind and waves

banks the sides of a river's channel

bayous streams that meander through a delta

bed the bottom part of a river's channel

bedrock the solid rock under the soil

bird's foot delta a delta built up along the different streams that enter the sea at the mouth of some rivers

bore a big wave that comes up a river from the sea during a special high tide

canalized to change a river by dredging, making it straighter, building locks and weirs and strengthening its banks

canyons very deep and steep-sided valleys (see gorges)

catchment area the area that is drained by a river and its tributaries (see drainage basin)

channels the bed and banks that contain a river's flow

conserved protected from unwanted, usually damaging, change

corrasion a rubbing action caused by stones in a river

dam a wall of rock, earth or concrete across a river

delta a natural shape made by deposited mud at the mouth of a river

discharge the amount of water flowing in a river

drainage basin the area drained by a river and its tributaries (see catchment area)

dredging digging out mud and other material from a river bed

energy the power used to do something

erosion the wearing away of rock and soil by water, wind or moving ice

estuary where a river widens out as it enters the sea

evaporate to change a liquid to a gas by heat

flash floods floods that happen very quickly, often as a result of a thunderstorm

flood when river water flows over a valley floor out of its normal channel

flood plain the bottom of a river valley that is sometimes flooded

food chain a set of feeding links between animals and vegetation

glacier a mass of ice moving down a valley

gorges very deep and steep-sided valleys (see canyons)

gradient a slope

hydro-electric power station a power station that works by using the force of flowing water to create energy

Ice Age a time when the Earth's climate was much colder than it is now

impermeable a material that does not allow water to sink through

inland drainage an area where rivers have no outlet to the sea

irrigation the watering of crops using artificial methods

levee a low natural wall on top of a river bank

lock a way to raise boats from one river or canal level to another

meander neck the narrow area of land between the start and end of a meander bend

meanders bends in a river's course

meltwater stream a stream that comes from a melting glacier

mouth the place where a river flows into the sea or another body of water

mudflats areas of mud at a river's mouth made up from the soil washed downstream

navigable a waterway suitable for boats to travel up and down

ox-bow lake a lake formed when a meander bend is cut off

permeable a material that water can sink through

plain a large area of fairly flat land

plunge hole a hole in the river bed at the bottom of a waterfall

polluted dirty

potholes holes in a river bed caused by the swirling action of stones

rapids a rocky stretch of a river that drops steeply and where the water currents are fast

reservoir an artificial lake behind a dam used to store water

resistant hard to wear away

rills small channels cut by flowing water

saturated soaked with water

sedimentary rocks rocks made from pieces of other rocks, vegetation and the remains of dead animals

sink hole a hole in the surface of limestone rock (see swallow hole)

source the point where a river starts

spring a place where water comes out of the ground

spurs ridges of high land that jut out into a valley

stalactites growths of redeposited limestone that hang down from a cave ceiling

stalagmites growths of redeposited limestone that grow up from a cave floor

stream a small river

surface runoff rainwater that flows off slopes into a stream

swallow hole a hole on the surface of limestone rock (see sink hole)

tidal the part of a river near the sea where the tide comes up the river channel at high tide

transpiration water that is breathed out by vegetation

tributary a river that flows into a larger river

valley a dip in the landscape created originally by river erosion

wadis dried up, steep-sided valleys in a desert

water table the level of water in rocks under the Earth's surface

water vapour water in the air as a gas

waterfalls places where running water drops vertically

weir an artificial waterfall to control a river's flow

white-water rafting the sport of going over rapids in a raft

Index

Numbers in plain type (4) refer to the text. Numbers in italic (9) refer to a caption.